From Grass to Bridge

Ben Nussbaum

✳ Smithsonian

Contributing Author

Allison Duarte, M.A.

Consultants

Tamieka Grizzle, Ed.D.
K–5 STEM Lab Instructor
Harmony Leland Elementary School

Ramiro Matos
Curator
Smithsonian

Publishing Credits

Rachelle Cracchiolo, M.S.Ed., *Publisher*
Conni Medina, M.A.Ed., *Managing Editor*
Diana Kenney, M.A.Ed., NBCT, *Content Director*
Véronique Bos, *Creative Director*
June Kikuchi, *Content Director*
Robin Erickson, *Art Director*
Seth Rogers, *Editor*
Mindy Duits, *Senior Graphic Designer*
Smithsonian Science Education Center

Image Credits: front cover, p.8, p.10, p.11 (all), p.12 (all), p.14, p.15, p.18, p.27 (bottom), p.32 © Smithsonian; p.5 (top) Glowimages/Getty Images; pp.6–7 (all) Public domain; p.13 Media Drum World/Alamy; p.16 imageBROKER/Alamy; p.17 (top) Prisma by Dukas Presseagentur GmbH/Alamy; p.19 Yendor Oz/Flickr; p.20 (left) Tom Salyer/Alamy Stock Photo; p.21 Xinhua/Alamy; p.22 (insert) Courtesy the Golden Gate Bridge, Highway and Transportation District; p.23 (insert) turtix/Shutterstock; p.26 Rob Crandall/Shutterstock; pp.26–27 Richard Gunion/Dreamstime; all other images from iStock and/or Shutterstock.

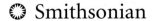

Smithsonian

Teacher Created Materials

5301 Oceanus Drive
Huntington Beach, CA 92649-1030
www.tcmpub.com

ISBN 978-1-4938-6687-8
© 2019 Teacher Created Materials, Inc.

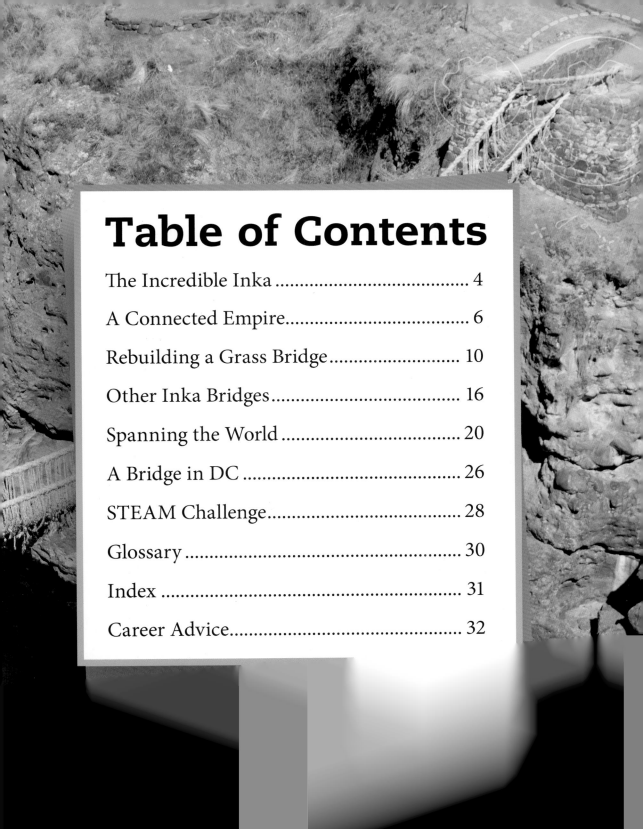

Table of Contents

The Incredible Inka

Hundreds of years ago, the Inka Empire was the largest empire on Earth. It stretched for more than 3,200 kilometers (2,000 miles) along the west side of South America.

The Inka were great builders. They had no iron or steel. They made palaces of stone and gold. They built cities on the sides of mountains. Their walls still exist in places that were part of their empire.

The Inka also used their building skills to create roads. Inka roads went up the Andes (AN-deez) Mountains and down into valleys. They crossed strong rivers. The roads let soldiers move quickly from place to place. People could send news faster. Farmers could bring food to big cities. Inka roads helped the empire run smoothly. The most impressive parts of the Inka roads were the bridges. Amazingly, some Inka bridges were made out of a simple resource. They were made from grass.

Some Inka structures are still standing.

This bridge connects two mountains in Peru.

A Connected Empire

The city of Cusco (KOOS-koh) can be found in Peru. Long ago, Cusco was the home of the Inka. At first, it was the only place the Inka controlled. Cusco was a city-state. There were many other city-states. Each one was like a small country. Each had its own leader.

Around 1400, the Inka wanted more land. Sometimes, they went to war to expand. Sometimes, other groups joined the Inka without war. The empire quickly took over a huge area.

The Inka built a vast system of roads. Together, all of these roads covered 40,234 km (25,000 mi.). That's enough to go from New York City to San Diego nine times.

The Inka Empire stretched between the west coast of South America and the Andes Mountains. It was long and skinny. Two main roads traveled north to south. One of these was near the coast. The other was in the mountains.

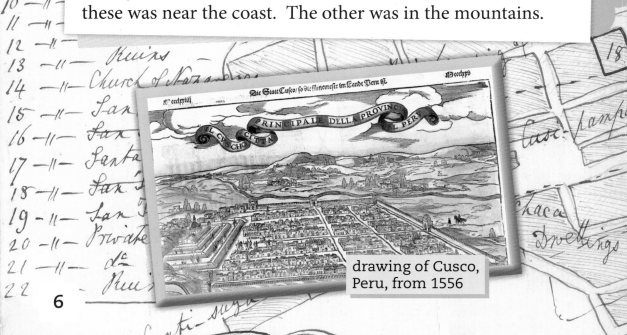

drawing of Cusco, Peru, from 1556

6

Cusco is still one of the largest cities in Peru.

The Inka did not use money. The government gave people food and clothes in exchange for goods and services.

7

Smaller roads connected the two main roads. Roads branched off toward many other places, too. Some were based on trails that existed before the Inka. The Inka created other roads themselves. The roads were designed based on the land around them.

In the desert, the roads were simple. The Inka marked paths and sometimes built low walls. They did not have to do anything else.

In the mountains, the Inka paved their roads. Snow and freezing cold would have destroyed simple roads. In hilly areas, they cut straight, flat roads. This took a lot of work, but it made walking easy.

In many areas, the Inka built walls on either side of the road to keep it flat and wide. Many of these walls are still standing.

The Inka also built bridges. About 200 bridges let the roads cross over canyons that were too steep to climb down.

Parts of the Inka road still exist.

The Inka used **llamas** to carry heavy loads. Llamas have soft feet, so the roads did not suffer too much wear and tear.

Rebuilding a Grass Bridge

Every June, villagers come together from both sides of the Apurímac (ah-poo-REE-mahk) River in Peru. They gather near a swinging grass bridge. It is called the Q'eswachaka (kes-wah-CHAH-kah) Bridge. Over the next few days, the villagers remake the bridge the way the Inka did hundreds of years ago. Women do some jobs, while men do others.

The bridge is a piece of living history. It has been in the same spot for at least 500 years. There was a lot of traffic on the bridge. It was also very long—29 meters (95 feet). It was among the longest of all the Inka bridges.

Making a new bridge starts with lots and lots of grass. Families work together to gather long stalks of grass called *ichu* (EE-choo). They dry the grass in the sun.

Then, women pound the grass with stones to soften it. They twist the grass into cords. The cords are like very thin, weak ropes. They are the basic building blocks for the bridge.

Grass is prepared to make into cords.

A woman prepares grass to be made into rope.

A modern bridge is near the grass bridge. People do not need to rebuild the grass bridge, but they do it because they are proud of their ancient Inka bridge.

Q'eswachaka Bridge

11

Men twist and braid the cords together to make strong rope. For the Q'eswachaka Bridge, 30 cords are used to form a single rope. These ropes are about as thick as a fist.

Next, men braid three ropes to make one thick cable. The cable is very strong. It is almost as thick as a soccer ball. Many cables are used for the floor of the bridge. Handrails on either side of the bridge are made by twisting two ropes together.

After a huge amount of grass has been twisted and braided, and the ropes and cables have been made, the dangerous work begins. The bridgemaster takes the lead. He is someone who has helped rebuild the bridge for years. He is the bridge's **architect**.

Using the old bridge, parts of the new bridge are carried over the canyon. Then, the old bridge is cut down. It crashes into the river and is swept away. Because it is grass, it does not pollute the river.

A woman twists grass into rope.

A man carries a handrail.

Stable Cables

Each of the cables in the Q'eswachaka Bridge must be able to carry about 454 kilograms (1,000 pounds). If not, the bridge will break when people use it. The cables have been tested, and they can each carry about 1,814 kg (4,000 lb.). That means the bridge is very stable.

It takes many people to help carry the cables into place.

People loop the thick cables and tie them to abutments. These are giant, strong stones with holes drilled into them by hand to allow cables to pass through. The abutments anchor the entire bridge. Small stone towers stand on either side of the bridge. Handrails and floor cables are tied to these towers.

The bridgemaster climbs onto the thick cables and sits down. His feet dangle on either side. Helpers crowd onto the bridge behind him. He ties the floor cables together. He also ties ropes between the handrail and the floor. This makes a wall that keeps people from falling off the bridge. Tying the handrails and floor together also makes the bridge more stable.

While the bridgemaster works from one side, another team works from the other side. They meet in the middle. Finally, a floor of sticks or mats is added to make sure that no one slips between the thick cables.

This team begins to work on their side of the bridge.

Bridge Basics

Tension is a pulling force. **Compression** is the opposite. It's a pushing force. Imagine a spring. When you pull the spring to make it longer, you create tension. When you push it together, you compress it. Both forces need to be balanced to create a stable bridge. A bridge is compressed as people walk across it. The cables holding it up create tension to balance the compression.

TENSION

COMPRESSION

The two teams meet in the middle of the bridge.

15

Other Inka Bridges

The Spanish who invaded the Inka Empire were used to short bridges made from stone. They were terrified of the **swaying** Inka bridges. Some of them crawled across on their hands and knees. They tried to replace the Inka bridges. They built huge stone bridges. Some of these collapsed. The deep, steep canyons of the Andes were too hard to cross.

Some Inka bridges remained in place for hundreds of years. Local people continued to rebuild them. They charged a **toll** to cross. Slowly, the Inka bridges were updated. Iron chain replaced rope. This made bridges much stronger. The stone towers that held the handrails were remade with **mortar**. This made them more stable.

Inka bridges are easiest to cross in the morning. Afternoons are windier, so the bridges sway more!

This bridge has iron abutments.

The Inka replaced most bridges every two or three years. The Q'eswachaka Bridge could not wait that long. It was replaced every year. The bridge was long and used by many people. It had to be very strong. It took about 250 people working for about two weeks to replace each bridge. One witness wrote that its cables were "as thick as a man's body."

Two bridges that crossed the Pampas River are also well known. In 1554, a writer described one of them. He said horses could gallop across the bridge. The other bridge was more fragile. He said mules had to be walked across one by one. That bridge was most likely made from thin, string-like fibers called fique (FEE-kay). Fique comes from a plant that grows in the area. A huge amount of twisting, weaving, and braiding was required to turn the fibers into thick, strong rope.

Cables are gathered to move into place.

The Long and Short of Bridges

A group of students at the Massachusetts Institute of Technology (MIT) made a rope bridge as a class project. They bought twine, a type of thin, weak rope. They made strong rope from the twine. The students made a bridge 18 m (60 ft.) long. They used 80 km (50 mi.) of twine to make the bridge.

Spanning the World

Hundreds of years ago, people made different kinds of bridges. They made bridges based on what they had to work with. They came up with smart ways to build bridges.

In one part of India, people made bridges from roots. Rubber trees grow roots above the ground. People guided these roots using hollow tubes. They guided the roots across rivers. Then, they let the roots grow into the ground on the other side. The roots grew into strong, sturdy bridges. Some of these bridges are still used.

The grass bridges of the Inka are a type of suspension bridge. That means they hang in the air. People in many places created suspension bridges. They used local plants. In Japan, some suspension bridges were made with thick vines. Some of these bridges are very popular sites for **tourists**.

In China, bridges were made with iron chain. This made them very strong.

iron chain bridge

root bridge

Some bridges today are built with glass floors. Walking on them is almost like floating on air!

21

Suspension bridges are still used, even though they may not look like the Inka bridges. The Golden Gate Bridge is a famous example of a suspension bridge. It is in California. Thick cables hang from giant towers. The cables dip in the middle. They are thick like the cables used by the Inka. Unlike the Inka, the cables for the Golden Gate Bridge are made from many thin strings of steel. Small cables hang from two main cables. The roadway connects to these small cables.

The load path of the Golden Gate Bridge starts with the roadway. *Load path* is an engineering term. It describes how weight is carried. Small cables support the roadway. The main cables support the small cables. Towers support the main cables. The towers go deep into the ground. They transfer all the weight to the earth. Huge **foundations** at both ends hold the cables tight.

Golden Gate Bridge during construction

Golden Gate Bridge

Why Orange?

When the Golden Gate Bridge was built in San Francisco, most bridges were painted black or gray. The bridge's designer wanted a color that would show off the bridge's details and size. Black paint would make those details hard to see. He wanted a color that would look good in both fog and bright sunlight. He wanted the bridge to be easy for ships and planes to see. Today, its orange color is **iconic**.

The bridges of the Inka are made from natural materials. When grass is cut, it grows back. Grass does not create pollution. It is not harmful.

Modern bridge builders are trying to be friendlier to the environment, too. One way is by adding **solar panels**. The Blackfriars Bridge in London is covered with these panels. The bridge is part of a busy train station. On a sunny day, the bridge supplies half the power that the station uses.

In Spain, the Sarajevo (sah-rah-YAY-voh) Bridge helps nature. It is covered with a special kind of concrete. The concrete breaks down pollution. It actually makes the air around the bridge cleaner. The Sarajevo Bridge also includes special walls where plants can grow.

In Montana in the United States, there is a bridge built just for animals. It is a wildlife crossing. This bridge goes over a busy highway. It is covered with dirt and plants. Animals stroll across without the risk of being hit by cars.

Blackfriars Bridge

TECHNOLOGY

Connecting Nature

Wildlife crossings may seem strange at first. Why would deer need a bridge? In truth, crossings can be very important. Many times, highways cut through habitats of local animals. Their homes may be on one side of the road, but their food and water sources are on the other. Without a wildlife crossing, animals are forced to cross a busy road. This can cause car accidents and hurt both people and wildlife.

A Bridge in DC

Each year, a festival is held in Washington, DC. It lasts for two weeks. It has a different theme each year. In 2015, the festival was all about Peru. Many people went to teach about their culture.

The builders of the Q'eswachaka Bridge were some of the people who went to the festival. They showed people how to weave and braid grass. They even built an 18-m (60-ft.) bridge with grass shipped from Peru! Many people came to watch. They learned about grass bridges. They also learned about Peru and the Inka.

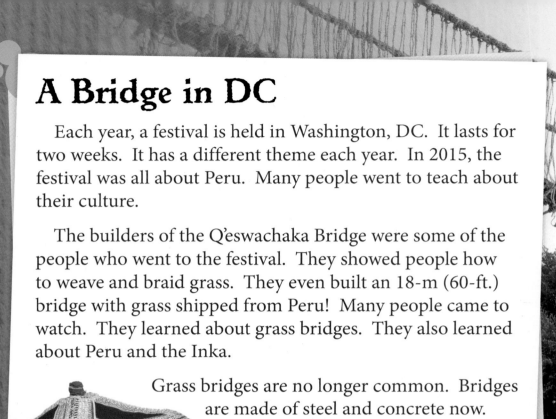

Grass bridges are no longer common. Bridges are made of steel and concrete now. But grass bridges are still important. Learning about them helps connect us to the past.

This woman from Cusco weaves at the festival.

This grass bridge was built at a festival in Washington, DC, in 2015.

Ropes are laid out to be made into cables.

27

STEAM CHALLENGE

Define the Problem

You are a civil engineer. The city planner seeks your advice on a new bridge. She has asked you to design a model of a bridge that will be used by cars, bikes, and travelers on foot. Use what you have learned about ancient and modern bridges to complete this task!

 Constraints: The bridge must extend 7 inches. You can use 200 craft sticks and a roll of tape to build your bridge.

 Criteria: Your bridge must be able to hold a textbook for 30 seconds.

Research and Brainstorm

What type of bridge will you build? Which part of a bridge must withstand the most force? Will you use all the materials available?

Design and Build

Sketch your bridge design. Include how many sticks you will use to build each part of the bridge. Where will you use the tape? Build the model. Make note of any changes you make to the plan.

Test and Improve

Test your bridge by setting a textbook on the bridge. Was the model successful? Did any part of the bridge fail during the test? How can you improve it? Modify your design, and try again.

Reflect and Share

Would more of either material improve the strength and stability? Could you make a successful bridge using fewer materials? What other forces do you think engineers consider when designing bridges?

Glossary

abutments—structures built to support the ends of a bridge

architect—a person in charge of planning a structure

compression—a pushing force

fique—a strong, natural fiber that grows in a plant found in and around Peru

foundations—the bases of structures

iconic—famous, legendary

llamas—four-legged animals, like horses or camels, but smaller

mortar—a substance that holds stones or bricks together

paved—covered with stones

solar panels—batteries that convert sunlight into electricity

swaying—shaking gently in the wind

tension—a pulling force

toll—a payment made to use a road or cross a bridge

tourists—people who go somewhere to take a vacation

Index

Do you want to help preserve the past?
Here are some tips to get you started.

"I am Quechua. We are descended from the Inka people. I am proud of the legacy the Inka left. I became an archaeologist because I am fascinated by learning from the past. If you also have a natural curiosity about history and all the people who came before us, then archaeology is the field for you!" —**Dr. Ramiro Matos, Curator, National Museum of the American Indian**

"Many people think of modern skyscrapers and large arenas as engineering marvels. However, architects often get ideas from the past. The Inka were master engineers. To learn about earlier people like the Inka, study history, geography, or anthropology. There's so much the Inka and other earlier cultures can teach us." —**Amy Van Allen, Project Manager, National Museum of the American Indian**